F U N
with
PAPIER MÂCHÉ

FUN
with
PAPIER MÂCHÉ

MARION ELLIOT

GOLDEN

A GOLDEN BOOK®

Western Publishing Company Inc, Racine, Wisconsin 53404

GOLDEN®, GOLDEN & DESIGN®, A GOLDEN BOOK®, AND A LITTLE GOLDEN BOOK®
are registered trademarks of Western Publishing Company Inc.
Published by Western Publishing Company Inc,
25-31 Tavistock Place, London WC1H 9SU.

© Salamander Books Ltd, 1994
129-137 York Way,
London N7 9LG,
United Kingdom.

ISBN 0-307-80809-2

CREDITS

Editor: Jilly Glassborow

Designer: Patrick Knowles

Photographer: Jonathan Pollock

Craft adviser: Leslie Thompson

Typeset by: SX Composing Ltd., Rayleigh, Essex

Colour separation by: Scantrans Pte. Ltd., Singapore

Printed in Belgium by: Proost International Book Production

Contents

INTRODUCTION

Papier mâché is great fun to make and just as much fun to paint afterwards. All you need are some old newspapers, PVA glue, petroleum jelly and an old paintbrush. Bowls and plates make perfect moulds, but you can also use balloons or make a mould from Plasticine or rolled-up newspaper. For safety, ask an adult to help you when a craft knife is needed, and never leave scissors lying open.

Papier mâché can be pasted on to Plasticine models

1 To make perfect papier mâché every time, follow these simple instructions. First, choose your mould. Then cover your work area with newspaper or an old plastic tablecloth. Pour some PVA glue into an old dish and thin it down with water.

2 If you are using a bowl or a plate as a mould, coat the surface with a thin layer of petroleum jelly to stop the paper from sticking to it.

Newspaper

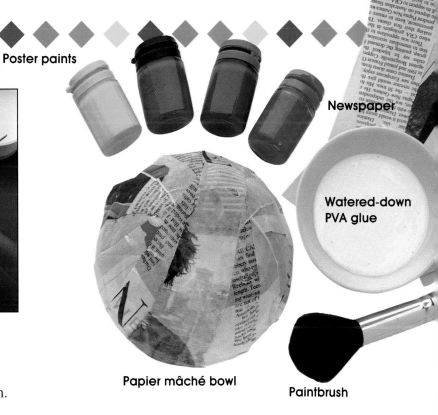

Watered-down
PVA glue

Papier mâché bowl

Paintbrush

3 Tear some newspaper into long narrow strips. Coat a strip with glue and paste it on to the mould. Continue to add strips, one at a time, overlapping them.

4 When your mould is completely covered, add about four more layers of paper in the same way. Then leave the papier mâché to dry in a warm place. Gently ease the cast off the mould and trim away any rough edges with a pair of scissors.

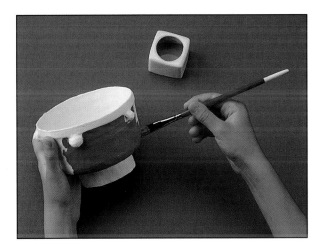

5 Paint your model white, using poster paint or emulsion. Now colour it with bright poster paints. Finally, give it two coats of varnish to protect the surface.

SUNNY SUNFLOWERS

Make yourself a bunch of cheerful sunflowers to brighten up your bedroom – unlike real flowers they'll never wilt and die. Start by tracing the flower pattern from page 30 using tracing paper and a pencil.

YOU WILL NEED

Cardboard

Strips of newspaper

Watered-down PVA glue

Garden sticks

Green crêpe paper

Green pipe cleaners

Tracing paper, pencil and scissors

Poster paints and paintbrushes

All-purpose glue

Clear varnish

Poster paints

1 Turn your trace face down on to the cardboard and rub firmly over the outline with your pencil. Cut out the flower shape and cover it with three layers of papier mâché. Add small lumps of papier mâché to the centre to make the seeds. Leave it to dry.

2 Glue the garden stick to the back of the flower to form the stem. Cover the join with a few more strips of papier mâché and leave it to dry.

3 Give your flower two coats of white paint. When the paint is dry, decorate it with orange and yellow poster colours and paint the seeds brown. Seal the colour with two coats of varnish.

4 Cut out two leaf shapes from green crêpe paper. Glue each leaf to the end of a pipe cleaner. Wrap the other end of the pipe cleaners round the flower stem as shown and glue them in place.

5 Cut a long strip of green crêpe paper 2cm (1in) wide. Starting at the top, neatly wrap it round the stick, covering the ends of the pipe cleaners as you go. Fix it in place at both ends with a dab of glue.

Glue

Paintbrush

Crêpe paper strip

Back of flower

Papier mâché seeds

Cardboard base

Leaf

Pipe cleaner

Scissors

Papier mâché flower

Garden stick

9

JAZZY BOWL AND PLATE

These brightly painted bowls and plates are easy to make using china tableware as moulds. For extra fun, decorate them with lumps of papier mâché round the rims, and make a stand for your bowl out of corrugated cardboard. Don't try to eat off them though – they're not water resistant.

YOU WILL NEED

Old china bowl and plate
Petroleum jelly
Strips of newspaper
Watered-down PVA glue
Cardboard
Masking tape
Gummed paper squares
Poster paints and paintbrushes
Clear varnish
Scissors

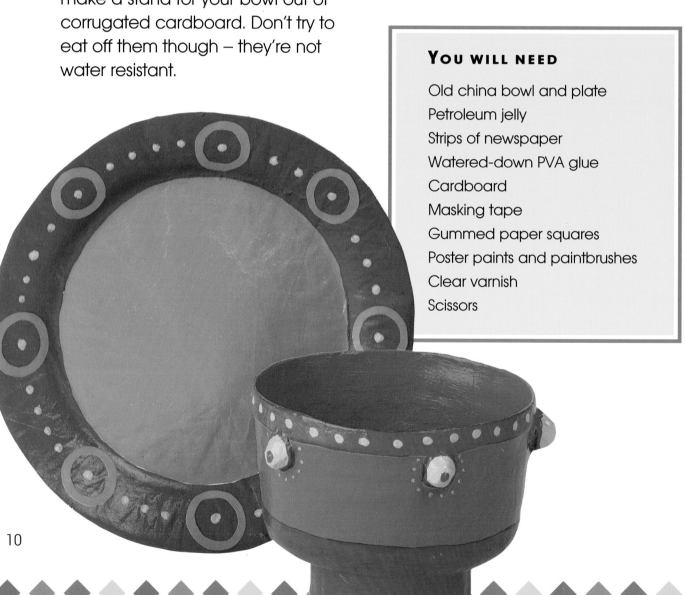

10

1. To make the plate, lightly coat the top of your china mould with petroleum jelly. Then cover it with four or five layers of papier mâché. If you like, decorate the rim with small bobbles of newspaper soaked in glue. Leave your plate to dry.

2. Gently ease the papier mâché away from the mould. Trim off any rough edges with your scissors to give a smooth edge. You can seal the rim with small strips of papier mâché if you want.

3. Make the bowl in the same way, covering the inside of your mould with papier mâché. Allow the bowl to dry before decorating it with bobbles of papier mâché pulp.

4. Cut a narrow strip of corrugated cardboard for the base. Ask an adult to help you cut into it on one side, as shown below, using a scissor blade. Attach the strip in a circle to the bottom of the bowl using masking tape. Then cover the base with papier mâché and leave it to dry.

5. Give your plate or bowl two coats of white paint, then decorate it with poster paints. Allow each colour to dry before applying the next. You can also cut shapes out of gummed paper squares and stick them on for decoration.

6. Finally, seal your bowl and plate with two coats of clear varnish.

Gummed
paper rings

Plate
mould

Trimming
edge of
plate

Papier mâché
bobbles

Papier
mâché
bowl

Masking
tape

Base

TIGER MASK

Go wild with this wonderful tiger mask. It's simple to make using a balloon as a mould and is bound to be a winner at any fancy dress party. Alternatively, you could make a lion by adding a mane of brown paper or replace the stripes with spots for a leaping leopard.

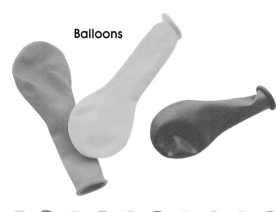

Balloons

12

1 Blow up your balloon so that it's as long as your face and slightly wider. Coat it with a thin layer of petroleum jelly and apply five layers of papier mâché.

2 When the papier mâché is thoroughly dry, pop the balloon with a needle. Then carefully cut the shape in half lengthways, using your scissors.

3 Using a pencil, trace the patterns for the nose and ears from page 30. You will need to trace the ear twice. Turn your trace face down on to the cardboard and retrace over the outlines. Cut out the card shapes.

4 Attach the ears to the top of the head with masking tape and glue the nose on to the centre of the face. Mark the position of the eyes with a felt-tip pen.

5 Cover the ears and nose with papier mâché and leave to dry. Then cut out the eyes with sharp pointed scissors, asking an adult to help if necessary.

6 Give the mask two coats of white paint. When it is dry, draw on the tiger's markings with a pencil and decorate your mask with bright poster paints. Seal with two coats of varnish.

7 Make a small hole at each side of the mask using a sharp pencil point. Thread round elastic through the holes, knotting the ends on the inside to keep the elastic in place.

Masking tape

Poster paints

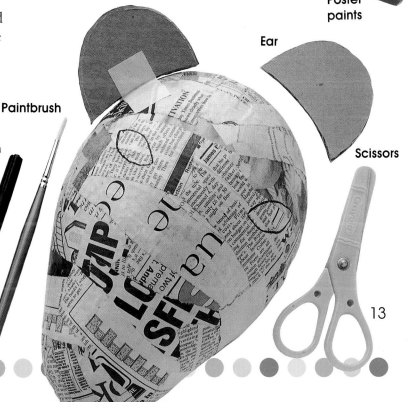

Round elastic

Nose

Pen

Paintbrush

Ear

Scissors

13

MARINE BOX

This pretty box is easily made by covering a cardboard frame with papier mâché. It is decorated with papier mâché pulp, forming a raised pattern of shells and fish, and makes the perfect container for jewellery, sewing equipment or secret possessions.

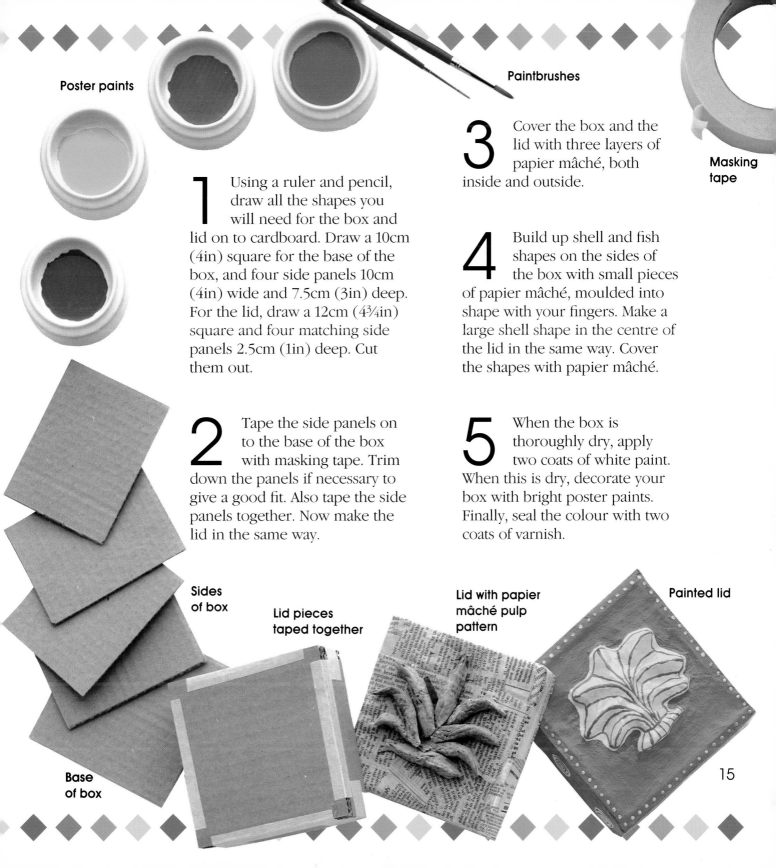

Poster paints

Paintbrushes

Masking tape

1 Using a ruler and pencil, draw all the shapes you will need for the box and lid on to cardboard. Draw a 10cm (4in) square for the base of the box, and four side panels 10cm (4in) wide and 7.5cm (3in) deep. For the lid, draw a 12cm (4¾in) square and four matching side panels 2.5cm (1in) deep. Cut them out.

2 Tape the side panels on to the base of the box with masking tape. Trim down the panels if necessary to give a good fit. Also tape the side panels together. Now make the lid in the same way.

3 Cover the box and the lid with three layers of papier mâché, both inside and outside.

4 Build up shell and fish shapes on the sides of the box with small pieces of papier mâché, moulded into shape with your fingers. Make a large shell shape in the centre of the lid in the same way. Cover the shapes with papier mâché.

5 When the box is thoroughly dry, apply two coats of white paint. When this is dry, decorate your box with bright poster paints. Finally, seal the colour with two coats of varnish.

Sides of box

Lid pieces taped together

Lid with papier mâché pulp pattern

Painted lid

Base of box

15

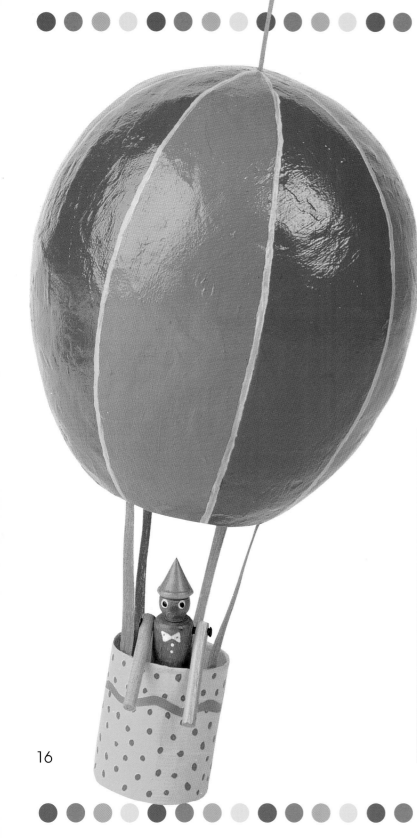

Hot-Air Balloon

Up, up and away! This beautiful balloon is made using a party balloon as a mould and a small dessert or fromage frais pot for the basket. It makes a wonderful decoration to hang from your bedroom ceiling. Put it in front of the window so you can watch it floating with the clouds.

You will need

Round balloon
Petroleum jelly
Strips of newspaper
Watered-down PVA glue
Small dessert carton
Paper ribbon
Felt-tip pen
Poster paints and paintbrushes
All-purpose glue
Clear varnish
Scissors

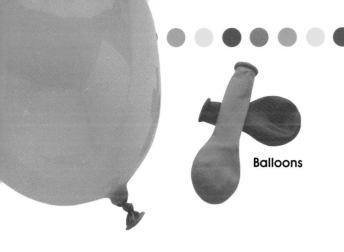
Balloons

4 Give the balloon and the basket two coats of white paint. When the paint is dry, decorate both pieces with poster paints. Seal the colour with two coats of clear varnish and leave to dry.

1 Blow up the balloon and tie the end in a knot. Thinly coat the balloon with petroleum jelly, then cover it in five layers of papier mâché. Leave it to dry in a warm place.

5 Ask an adult to cut a small slit in the top of the balloon. Thread a length of paper ribbon through and secure it in place on the inside of the balloon with a dab of glue. Use this ribbon to hang up your balloon.

Paintbrushes

2 If necessary, trim the edge of the dessert carton with scissors to neaten it. Cover the carton with two or three layers of papier mâché to make the little basket.

6 Finally, cut four lengths of ribbon and glue one end of each piece to the inside of the balloon. Attach the other ends to the inside of the basket, making sure that the basket hangs evenly.

Poster paints

3 When the papier mâché is dry, pop the balloon. Draw a circle round the base as shown and cut it out with your scissors.

Papier mâché shell

Paper ribbon

Glue

Dessert carton

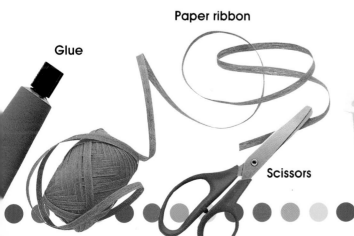

Scissors

17

Dynamic Dinosaurs

Return to pre-historic times with these handsome model dinosaurs. Display them in your bedroom to scare away unwelcome intruders! No one really knows what colour dinosaurs were, so you can paint yours in bright jazzy colours.

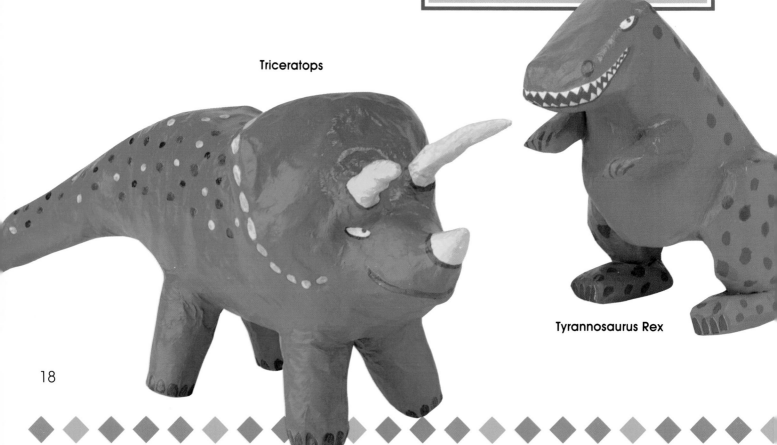

Triceratops

Tyrannosaurus Rex

18

1 Make the basic dinosaur shape by folding, rolling and squashing sections of newspaper into shape as shown below. Bind the newspaper with masking tape to keep it in place. Make the arms and legs in the same way and tape them into position on the body.

2 Cover your dinosaur model with four of five layers of papier mâché, overlapping the strips as you go. Then leave the dinosaur to dry in a warm place overnight.

3 When the papier mâché is thoroughly dry, apply two coats of white paint, allowing the first coat to dry before applying the second.

4 Draw on the dinosaur's features, such as the eyes and mouth, using a pencil. Then colour in your design with poster paints. You may have to apply two coats of paint to get a good, even finish. Finish off with plenty of brightly coloured spots all over the dinosaur's back.

5 When the paint is thoroughly dry, apply two coats of clear varnish to seal the colour.

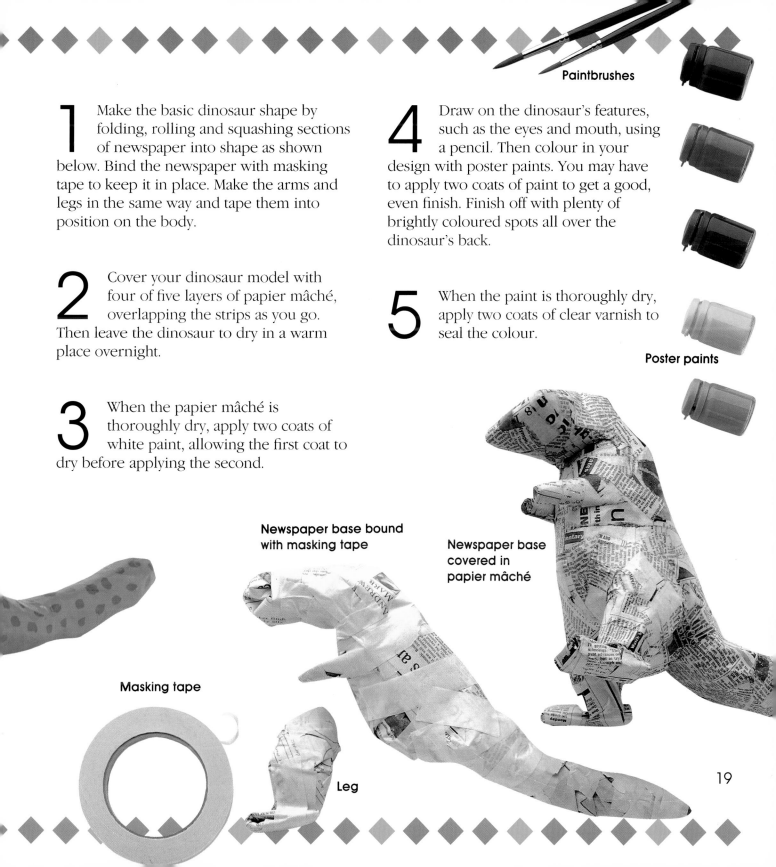

Paintbrushes

Poster paints

Newspaper base bound with masking tape

Newspaper base covered in papier mâché

Masking tape

Leg

19

PIGGY BANK

Make saving fun by creating this speckled pink piggy bank to hold your money. His body is moulded round a balloon, and his nose and legs are made from toilet rolls.

YOU WILL NEED

Round balloon

Strips of newspaper

Watered-down PVA glue

Petroleum jelly

3 toilet rolls

Cardboard

Pink pipe cleaner

Wine bottle cork

All-purpose glue

Masking tape and scissors

Poster paints and paintbrushes

Ruler and pencil

Clear varnish

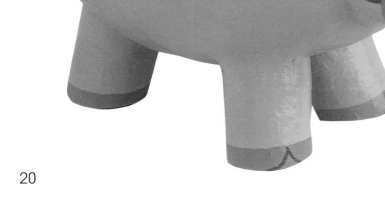

1 Blow up the balloon and thinly coat it with petroleum jelly. Cover it with five to six layers of papier mâché, leaving a slit at the top for the money and a hole in the bottom for the cork.

2 Leave the papier mâché in a warm place to dry. Then pop the balloon and remove it.

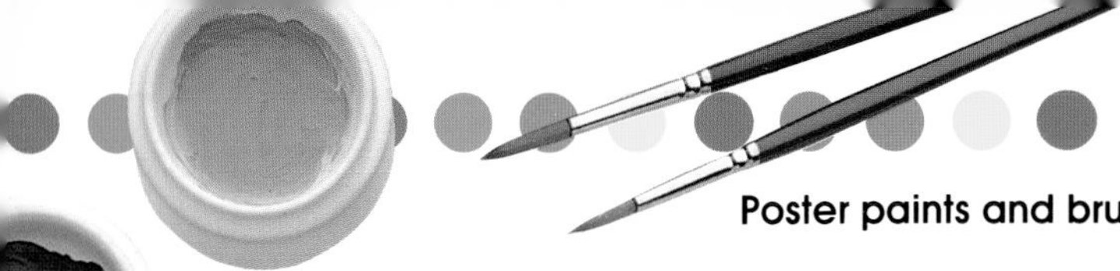

Poster paints and brushes

3 Cut two of the toilet rolls in half to make the legs. Cut them at an angle so that they fit snuggly against the pig's tummy.

4 Cut the remaining toilet roll in half to make the nose. Place one half end-down on the cardboard and draw round it. Cut out the circle and tape it to the end of the nose. Tape the legs and nose to the body as shown below.

5 To make the ears, cut two triangles from cardboard. Ask an adult to help you cut two slits in the pig's head. Slot in the ears and tape them in place. Bend the tops of the ears over.

6 Ask an adult to help you neaten the coin slot and cut the hole to fit the cork using sharp pointed scissors. Paste extra papier mâché on to the nose, legs and ears, and leave it to dry.

7 Give your pig two coats of white paint. Then paint it pink with big brown splodges. Paint on hooves, eyes and nostrils using a fine brush.

8 Wrap the pipe cleaner round a pencil to make a curly pink tail. Make a small hole in the pig with the point of a sharp pencil and glue the tail into the hole. Coat your pig with two coats of varnish to seal the colour.

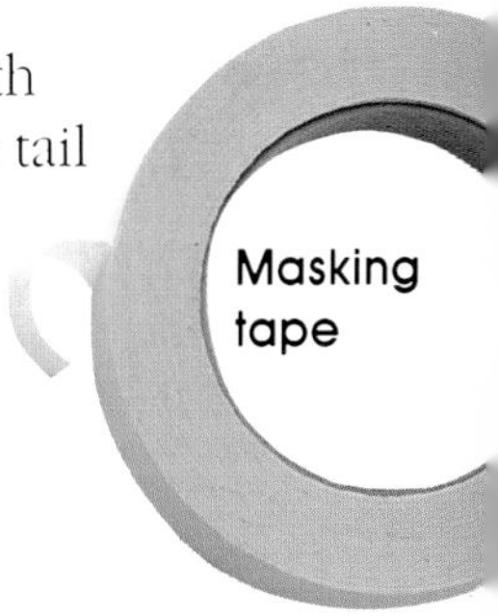

Masking tape

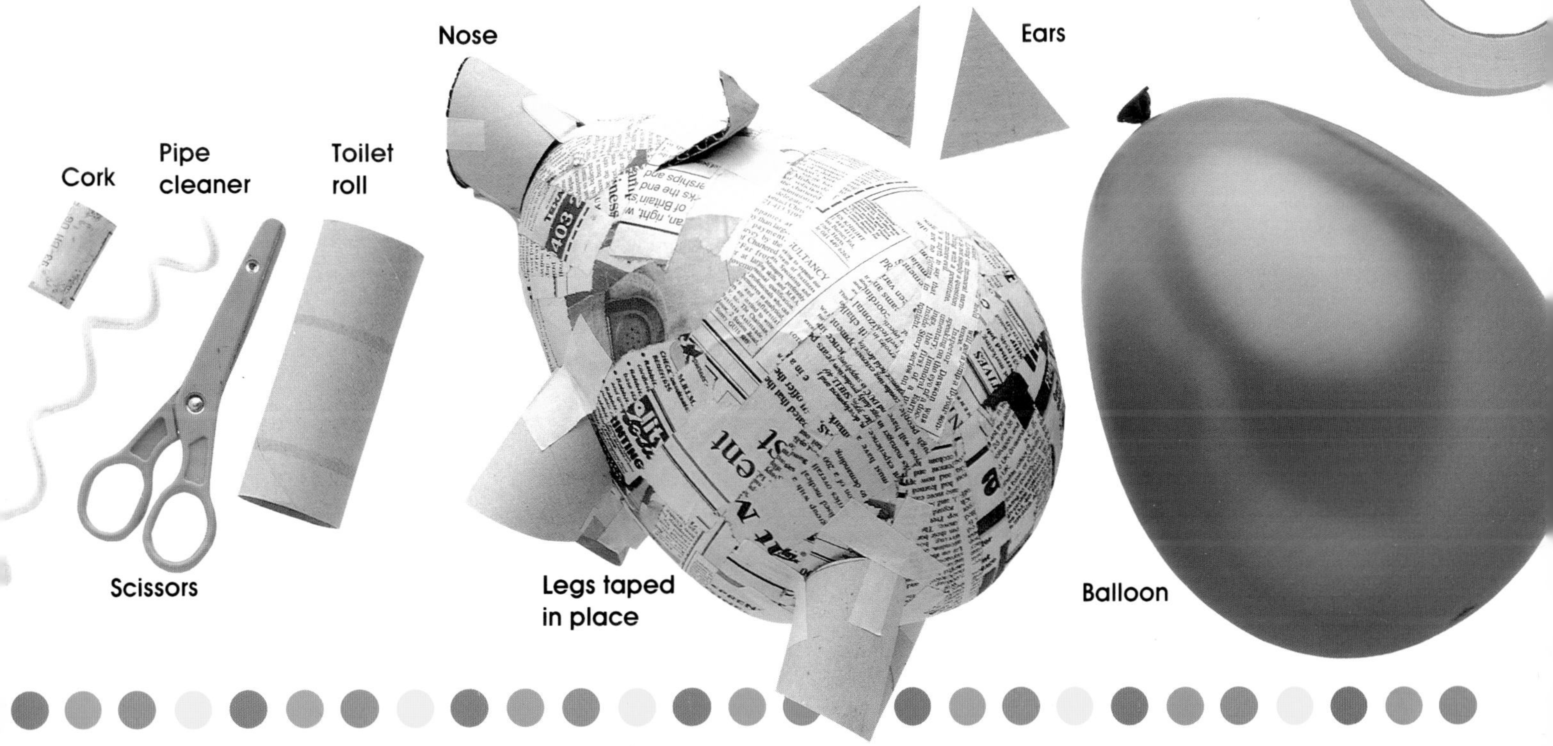

Nose

Ears

Cork

Pipe cleaner

Toilet roll

Scissors

Legs taped in place

Balloon

BREAKFAST TIME

What better way to start the day than with these chirpy chickens? To create these novelty egg cups, make a Plasticine mould and simply cover it with papier mâché. The egg cups can't be washed, but you can wipe them over with a damp cloth to keep them clean.

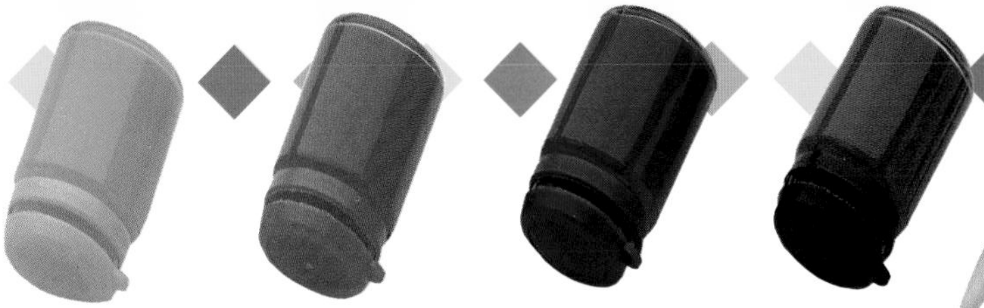

Poster paints

Paintbrush

Pencil

1 Knead the Plasticine in your hands until it is soft and smooth. Then mould it into a chicken shape with your fingers and a modelling tool.

2 Use your modelling tool to carve a hole in the chicken's back, popping an egg into the hole to make sure it's the right size. Give your chicken a large flat base so that it stands up easily.

3 Cover your model with four layers of papier mâché. Then leave it to dry in a warm place.

4 Ask an adult to cut lengthways all the way round the papier mâché shell with a craft knife. Then carefully prize the two halves apart with a blunt knife and scoop out all the Plasticine (as shown below) to give two hollow shells.

5 Rejoin the two halves with masking tape and cover the join with small pieces of papier mâché.

6 When the papier mâché is dry, give the model two coats of white paint. Draw on the chicken's features using a pencil and then colour in your design with bright poster paints.

7 Finally, when the paint is dry, give your model two coats of clear varnish to seal the colour.

Egg

Masking tape

Plasticine mould covered in papier mâché

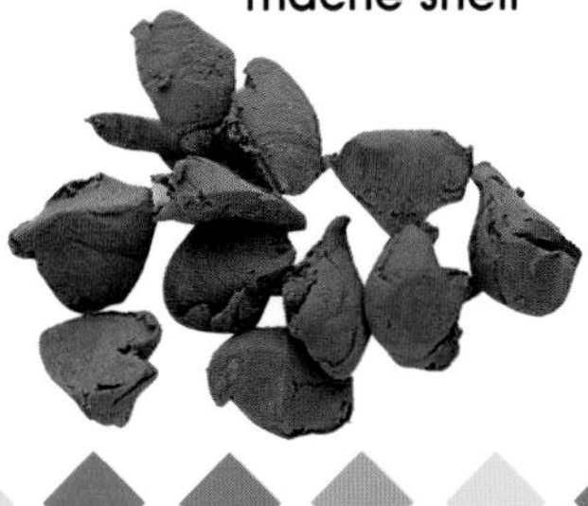

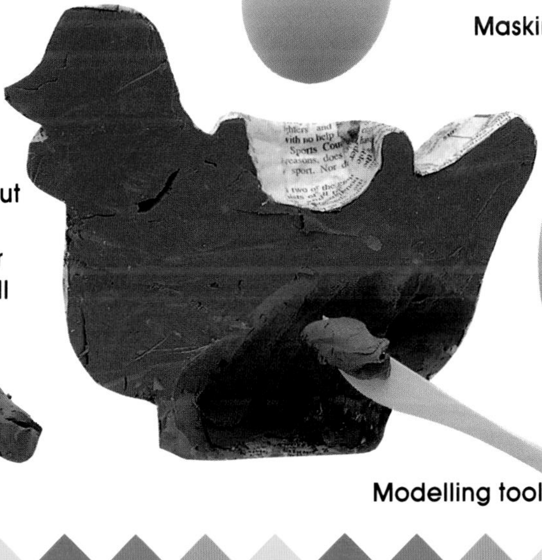

Scooping out Plasticine from papier mâché shell

23

Modelling tool

Heidi Doll

This jolly dolly is made with tightly folded and rolled newspaper covered in papier mâché. Her limbs are joined to her body with small metal loops called eye pins. These can be bought from craft and hobby shops.

You will need

Newspaper
Watered-down PVA glue
Masking tape
Poster paints and paintbrushes
All-purpose glue
Clear varnish
Tracing paper and pencil
8 eye pins
Red, white and blue felt
Yellow wool
Needle and thread
Dressmaker's pins
Darning needle
Scissors

1 Make the doll's body by folding sheets of newspaper into an oblong 15cm × 7.5cm (6in × 3in), and about 2.5cm (1in) thick. Bind the oblong together with masking tape.

Paints and brush

Masking tape

Glue

Wool loops

2 Make a small oblong for the head and tape it to the body. Make arms and legs by rolling newspaper into tubes and taping the ends. Add small feet to the legs.

3 Cover all the pieces with four layers of papier mâché, building up the face with extra layers. Leave the pieces to dry.

4 Give all the pieces two coats of white paint, then paint them pink. Add the features with a fine brush and seal with two coats of clear varnish.

5 With an adult's help, make a small hole in the top of the arms and legs with a darning needle, and matching holes in the sides and base of the body. Glue an eye pin into each hole. Open out the loops on the leg pins and hook them on to the body. Close up the loops.

6 Form the wool into loops about 25cm (10in) long and glue it on to the doll's head. Trim the ends and plait the wool on each side, tying off with a little wool.

7 Trace the blouse pattern from page 31 and cut it out. Pin the pattern on to two layers of blue felt. Cut out the felt and sew them together along the shoulder and side seams. Glue strips of white felt on to the blouse and put it on the doll.

8 Cut two pieces of red felt 20cm × 10cm (8in × 4in) for the skirt. Sew the two short sides together. Stitch around the top of the skirt, leaving the thread ends loose. Slide the skirt on to the doll and pull the thread tight to gather the skirt. Finally, attach the arms as before.

Skirt

Thread

Blouse

Legs

Arms

Newspaper base

Needle

Eye pins

25

CIRCUS SKITTLES

This trio of circus characters is moulded around plastic drink bottles that have been weighed down with sand. Use a soft ball to throw at your skittles so you don't damage them.

YOU WILL NEED

Empty plastic drink bottles

Strips of newspaper

Watered-down PVA glue

Sand

Masking tape and scissors

Cardboard and stiff paper

Poster paints and paintbrushes

All-purpose glue

Clear varnish

Pencil

Poster paints

Paintbrush

Pencil

PVA glue

1 Pour sand into a plastic drink bottle until the bottle is about a third full. Put the lid back on.

2 Cover the bottle with three layers of papier mâché. Build up the head shape with small lumps of papier mâché, smoothing it down with your fingers.

3 For each skittle, draw two arms on to cardboard, following the shapes shown below. Draw dumbells in the weightlifter's hand. Cut out the arms and tape them on to the skittles.

4 Make the clown's hat by cutting a section out of a circle of stiff paper. Fold it into a cone shape and tape the overlapping edges together. Tape the hat on to the clown's head.

5 Make the ringmaster's hat out of a small cylinder of cardboard and tape a circle of card to each end. Don't put the hat on the skittle just yet.

6 Cover the arms and the clown's hat with small pieces of papier mâché. Also cover the points where they join the body. Now cover the ringmaster's hat with papier mâché. Leave to dry.

7 Give the skittles two coats of white paint. When this is dry, draw on the features with a pencil, then colour them in using poster paints. Seal with two coats of clear varnish.

8 Finally, glue the hat on to the ringmaster's head with strong glue.

Arm

Weightlifter's arm

Drink bottle mould with sand inside

Sand

Scissors

Clown's hat

Top hat

Masking tape

NAUTICAL PUPPETS

Jolly Jack tar and his mermaid friend are full of fun. Their papier mâché heads are made on Plasticine moulds and their bodies are made of felt.

YOU WILL NEED

1 large pack of Plasticine

Strips of newspaper

Watered-down PVA glue

Modelling tool and blunt knife

Craft knife (for adult use only)

Poster paint and paintbrushes

All-purpose glue

Tracing paper and pencil

Squares of coloured felt

Needle, thread and pins

Blue and yellow ribbon

Yellow wool

Scissors

1 Knead the Plasticine in your hands until it is soft and smooth. Then mould it into the shape of the head, adding the hat for the sailor. Make the neck 5cm (2in) in diameter.

Paintbrush

Poster paints

Plasticine

Wool for hair

Felt

2 Cover the head with five layers of papier mâché and leave it in a warm place to dry. Then ask an adult to cut all the way round the papier mâché shell with a craft knife. Prize the two halves apart with a blunt knife and dig out the Plasticine (as shown below) to give two hollow shells.

3 Cut away the base of the neck and join the two halves together with masking tape. Cover the join with papier mâché. When it is dry, give the head two coats of white paint. Then paint it pink (except the hat) and add the features.

4 Trace the patterns for the clothes on pages 31 and 32, completing the body patterns as marked. Cut out all the pieces and pin them on to the felt. Cut out all the felt shapes – you will need two bodies and four hands.

5 Sew the clothes together (as marked on the pattern) along the top and side seams. Leave the wrists and neck open, checking that the head fits inside the neck opening. Sew the hands together in pairs, then sew them into the wrist openings.

6 Sew or glue the bib on to the front of the sailor's body, adding strips of white felt. Cut out two felt shell shapes and some yellow and green scales and glue them on to the mermaid.

7 Glue the felt body to the papier mâché head. Tie a length of ribbon around the sailor's hat and measure out several lengths of wool for the mermaid's hair. Glue this to the mermaid's head, adding little yellow bows to make a pony tail.

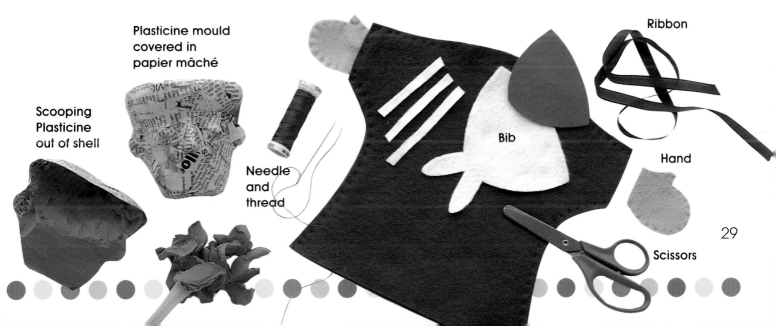

Plasticine mould covered in papier mâché

Scooping Plasticine out of shell

Needle and thread

Bib

Ribbon

Hand

Scissors

29

PATTERNS

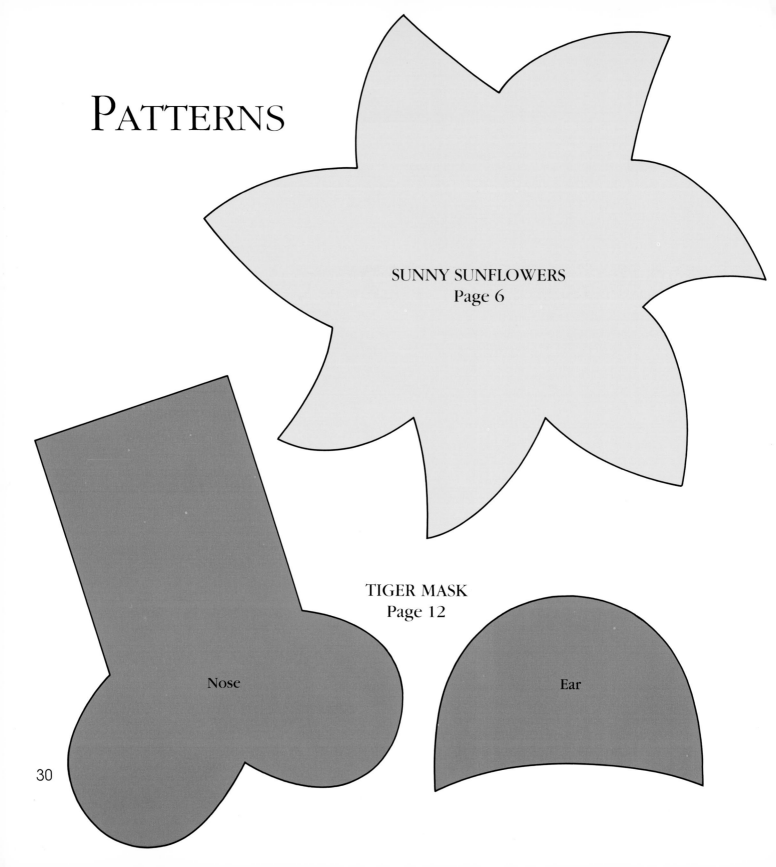

SUNNY SUNFLOWERS
Page 6

TIGER MASK
Page 12

Nose

Ear

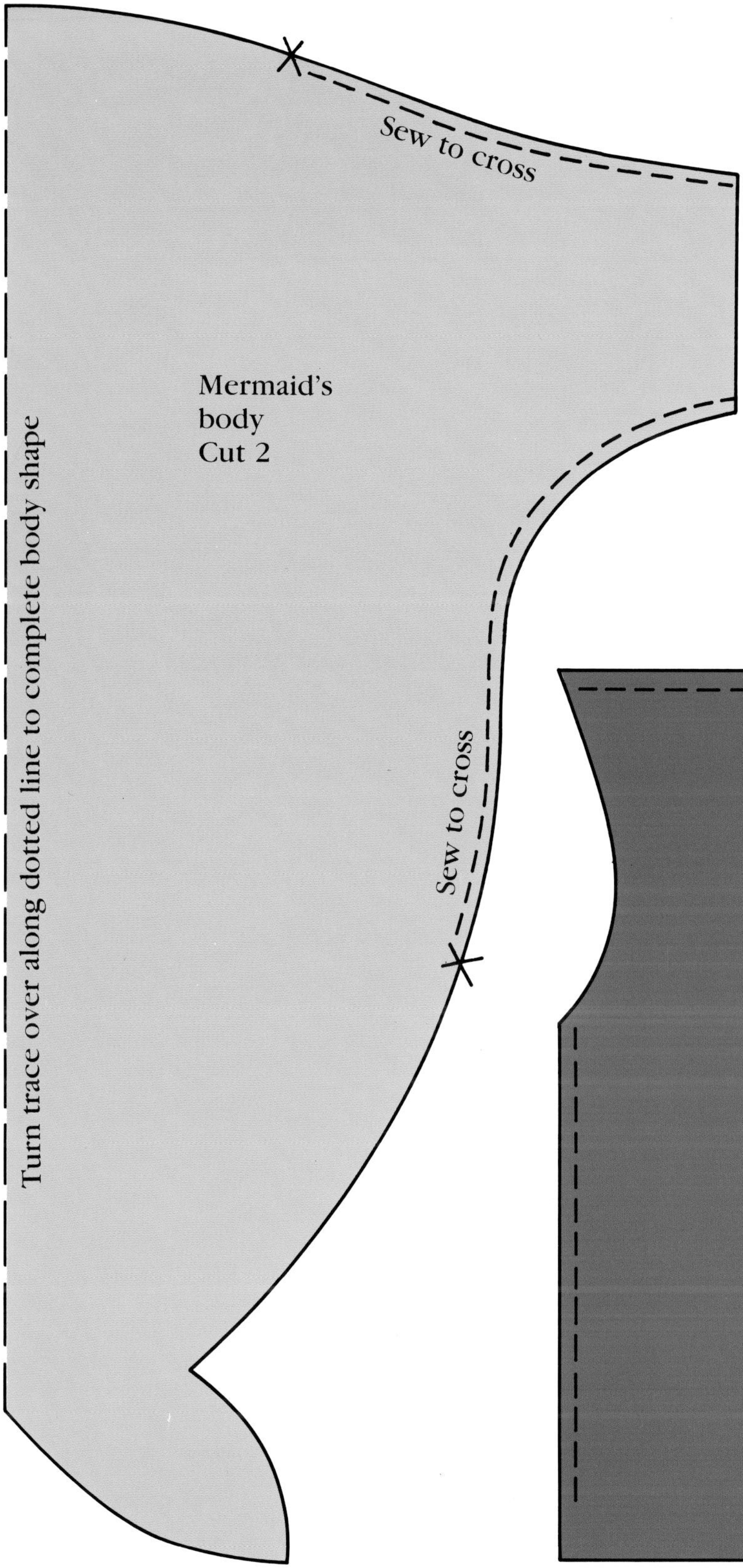

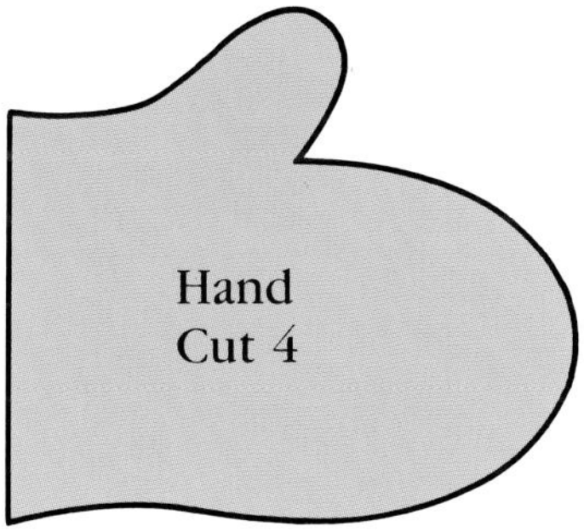

Sew to cross

MERMAID PUPPET Page 28

Hand
Cut 4

Mermaid's
body
Cut 2

Turn trace over along dotted line to complete body shape

Sew to cross

HEIDI DOLL Page 24

Blouse
Cut 2

31

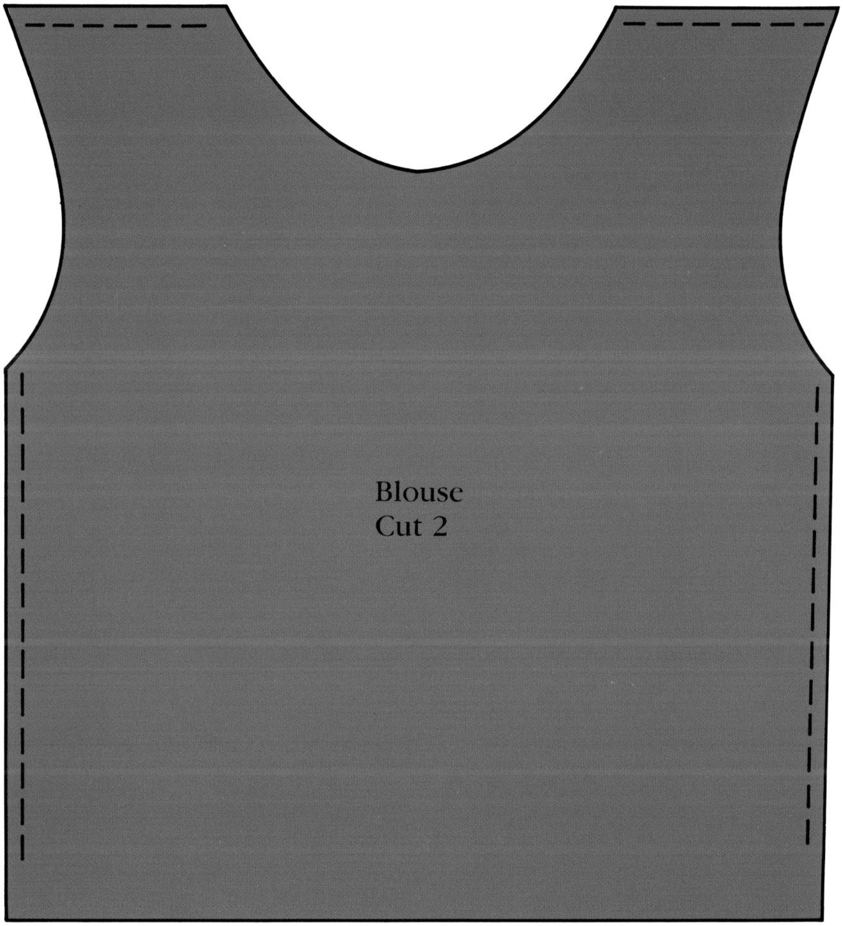

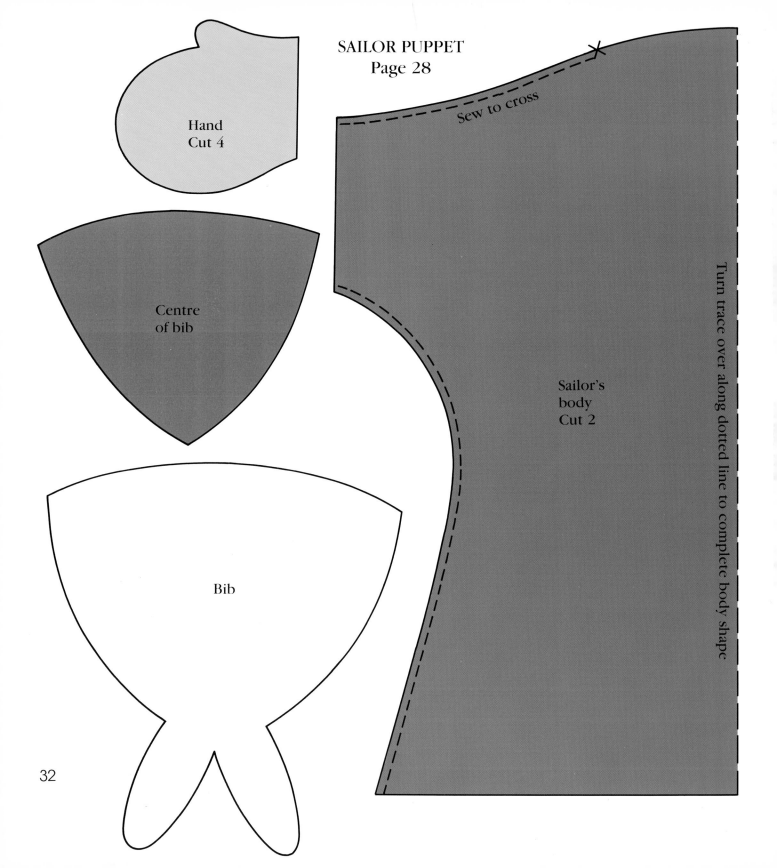

SAILOR PUPPET
Page 28

Hand
Cut 4

Centre
of bib

Bib

Sew to cross

Sailor's
body
Cut 2

Turn trace over along dotted line to complete body shape